Welcoming

Happiness

"A guide to finding more peace, hope, joy and balance in life."

Sakariya Hirad

Welcoming Happiness: A Guide to Finding More Peace, Hope, Joy, and Balance in Life

Copyright © 2025 by Sakariya Hirad.

ISBN: 979-8-9936592-0-6

Introduction

Discover the keys to living a fuller, happier, and more meaningful life in *Welcoming Happiness: A Guide to Finding More Peace, Hope, Joy, and Balance in Life*. This book is a heartfelt guide to mastering your thoughts, emotions, and actions, helping you welcome joy, peace, and abundance into your life. From cultivating courage and faith, to embracing self-love, gratitude, and positivity, each chapter empowers you to take control of your mindset, your habits, and your happiness.

Filled with practical wisdom, raw honesty, and timeless truths, this book will teach you how to:

- Step out of your head and take action despite fear

- Focus on the good and practice gratitude daily

- Maintain balance, healthy limits, and self-care

- Cultivate faith, hope, and resilience in life's challenges

- See the silver lining, find opportunities in difficulties, and grow from every experience

- Love yourself, love others, and live authentically

- Harness the power of your thoughts, beliefs, and manifestation

Whether you're seeking guidance, inspiration, or a motivational call to live life more intentionally, this book will help you reclaim your present, embrace your humanity, and create the life you've always wanted. *Your journey toward inner peace, self-discovery, and true happiness starts here.*

Table of Contents

Acknowledgements

S hout out to my mama and my daddy that looked out for me, did soo much for me, extended me a lot of grace, stood by my side no matter what, and still do. Thankful for my family, my friends, my peers. Thank you to everybody who spreads kindness. Thankful for all the love and support in the world. Thankful for the staff that let me get computer access even though I'm incarcerated. Thankful for my recovery, therapy, and rehabilitation. Thankful for the abundance/plentiness of good in life.

Dedications

This book is dedicated to the world without people this wouldn't have been possible. People are love, people are joy with touches of imperfections, LOL. So, to everybody, I hope you enjoy and I wish us all the absolute very best.

Chapter 1: Welcoming Happiness

So here it is. Instead of doing things and taking action with the mindset that you *must* get happiness as a guaranteed result, shift your intention. Don't chase happiness like it's owed to you—welcome it. Create space for it. You are the master of your intent.

Take action in ways that align with what you want for your life. When your actions and intentions line up, you naturally invite the peace, joy, and happiness you desire. But here's the key—avoid 100% expectation. When you expect happiness like a promise, you set yourself up for disappointment. Life doesn't always go the way we plan.

Maybe it'll happen, maybe it won't. If it does, you'll enjoy it even more because you weren't gripping it with the tight fist of expectation. If it doesn't, you won't feel crushed—you'll still be at peace. This is how you welcome happiness, instead of demanding it.

Believe that there is always a high possibility for good things to come your way. You can only achieve what you allow yourself to believe is possible. If in your mind something is impossible, you've already blocked yourself from it. But when you choose to believe—even if it's just a little—that good things are likely, then you open the door.

Believe in the possibility of joy. Believe in the possibility of peace. Believe in the possibility of positive change. When you choose to see life as a place where good things can and will happen, you create the conditions for those good things to flow toward you.

Welcome happiness. Don't chase it. Don't force it. Open the door to it every day through your actions, your mindset, and your faith that it is possible.

Chapter 2: Acceptance

It can be difficult at times to accept things as they are, especially when we want them to be exactly the way we envisioned. But remind yourself: "It's okay that things aren't going exactly the way I wanted or planned."

Practice radical acceptance of the following truths:

Life wasn't meant to be all perfect.

Life wasn't meant to go your way all the time.

Life wasn't meant to be all ease.

Life wasn't meant to be entirely fair.

Life wasn't meant to be entirely heavenly.

Life was meant to be life.

However, life is still a blessing — see the good in everything.

Accept that we were meant to be human, not perfect. We were meant to be flawed, to make mistakes, and sometimes to do wrong. Our brains aren't always positive, and our thoughts and feelings won't always align with us, our values, our beliefs. Accept not all thoughts are true, and that you are not all your thoughts.

Accept that we all carry different flaws, imperfections, views, beliefs, thoughts, mindsets, experiences, likes and dislikes, feelings, desires, strengths, and weaknesses. Accept that we won't always agree — and that's okay.

In life, you'll find yourself in situations where it's best to do something you don't feel like doing. That, too, is part of the imperfections of this world.

It's important to frequently remind ourselves of acceptance — and that it's okay. We tend to forget sometimes, and that's okay too. It's all just part of our humanity. Be accepting of your humanness and treat yourself with loving-kindness.

Acknowledge there's many right paths, Accept that your way isn't the only right way. Accept that we're all unique — and just because something is right or works for you doesn't mean it's right or will work for everyone.

Not everybody is meant for you. That doesn't mean they're against you — they're just not for you. And guess what? You don't need the approval of people who aren't for you. The Higher Power provides you with everyone you need. You just have to believe, and open your eyes to see it.

It's not just about what's or who's right — it's about what's right **for you**. Give others the love and freedom to do them, just like you want the freedom to do you.

Accept that people won't always behave the way you want them to. Accept that things won't always go your way. That's just life.

God created us all to be unique. We weren't meant to be exactly the same.

Accept that everyone has their own challenges and limitations. Accept that we're all equal, and that everyone is just as important as anyone else.

Without the cashier, the fast-food cook, the janitor, or the warehouse worker — how would the world function? The world would crumble without them. Every role matters. Every presence matters. You get the point: we all have different roles, but every presence is just as important as anybody else's. Be humble. Be loving. Be free. Be light hearted.

Chapter 3: Purpose and Meaning

It really doesn't have to be complicated. Purpose is something people often overthink, like it has to be this grand mission or something that changes the whole world. But truth is, your purpose can be as simple as you want it to be. It could be to do good. It could be to help people. It could be to live a life of service. It could be to just be yourself, or to take care of your family. It doesn't need to be extra or flashy—it just needs to feel right for you.

The most important part is that your **heart is invested** in it. If your heart's not in it, it's not purpose, it's just obligation. Don't live trying to meet other people's expectations—live in a way that adds meaning to *your* life. Nobody else can define what makes your life meaningful. That answer is already inside you.

Joseph Campbell said, *"Follow your bliss and the universe will open doors where there were only walls."* That's the truth. When you follow what really matters to you, life opens up.

So do the things you actually want to do. Go after the desires that light you up. There is no law written in the sky saying you're supposed to live a certain way. This is your life—live it how you want, in a way that brings you joy.

Chapter 4: Kindness and Giving

I can't put enough emphasis on how important kindness is. Even the small acts—the little things you do for yourself and for others—matter more than you think. A kind word, a smile, your time, your company, your service, your food, your money, your grace, your empathy, your love, your prayer, your acceptance, your gratitude, your open-mindedness, your understanding... the list goes on. There are countless ways to be kind and to give.

But here's the thing: do it for the sake of kindness itself—not to get something back in return. The satisfaction of doing it just to do it, for no reward, is already enough. That's where the real beauty is.

Of course, be responsible with your giving. Set healthy limits. Don't drain yourself dry trying to please or fix everyone—that's not kindness, that's self-neglect. True kindness always includes yourself too.

So, treat yourself with loving-kindness. With grace. With forgiveness. Yes, you'll slip up. Yes, you'll make mistakes. Yes, you've got flaws and weaknesses. But all of that is just a small piece of the bigger picture. You're enough as you are, right now. You're okay just as you are.

And even when you don't feel like it, you still deserve kindness. We all do. Nobody chose to be imperfect. Nobody asked to be prone to messing up. But here we are—flawed humans who still deserve love, grace, and compassion.

So spend as much kindness as you can—toward strangers, toward loved ones, and toward yourself—even on your hard days.

And while we're on it: avoid criticizing, condemning, nitpicking, and fault-finding. Those things only bring you down and push people away. They hurt more than they help. Instead, lean into joy, into words that uplift, into actions that heal. If you do criticize, let it be constructive, let it be lighthearted, let it be laced with humor and never too heavy.

For the most part, speak with love. Speak with joy. Move through life with kindness as your currency. Because when you give kindness, you invite more love, joy, and good things into your life.

We are all—every single one of us—positively, humbly powerful.

Chapter 5: Empathy and Understanding

It's in our human nature to be judgmental. Sometimes it feels automatic, almost like instinct. Maybe that's because judgment is something we've been practicing for so long that it's become a habit. But habits can be broken. Instead of letting yourself automatically judge, start training yourself to lean toward understanding. Shift the cycle. Seek progress, not perfection.

Empathy isn't just for others—it's also for yourself. It's about choosing to pause, to try to see from another perspective, even when you don't agree. Everybody wants to feel understood, just like you do. And when you show people that you understand them, they feel seen, they feel valued, and they're much more likely to want to understand you too.

Have grace with your mistakes, and with the mistakes of others. Remember: we weren't created to be flawless. We weren't designed to never slip up. Humanity is messy by nature, and that's okay. Allow yourself and others room for error. Be understanding. Be graceful. Look beyond someone's behavior—see the whole person, the bigger picture of their humanity.

And while empathy is powerful, it also needs balance. Keep your emotional involvement at healthy levels. You don't have to carry every burden to be understanding. You don't have to drown in someone else's emotions to empathize. Sometimes just listening, just seeking to understand, is enough.

The way you interpret a situation often determines how you feel about it. Choosing to give someone the benefit of the doubt, or to lean toward a positive, compassionate perspective, will always feel better than sinking into negativity or judgment.

We all carry different flaws, challenges, and limitations. We all make mistakes—but none of that gives anyone the right to condemn or resent another person just because they're different. At the core, we are all the same: human. Equal. Part of the same family of humanity.

Having more than someone else doesn't make you superior. Being blessed in a certain area doesn't make you above anybody. At the end of the day, no matter what you have, no matter what you lack, you're still human— and so is everyone else. We share struggles, we share emotions, we share life itself.

The only true Superior is God. He has no flaws. Every blessing you have comes from Him, and just as easily as He gave it to you, He can give it to someone else. We all carry incredible potential. We are all capable of greatness.

So, instead of judgment, choose empathy. Instead of condemnation, choose understanding. Instead of resentment, choose grace. That choice not only uplifts others—it frees you too.

Chapter 6: Managing Thoughts, Emotions, and Behaviors

Life is a web where situations, environments, thoughts, emotions, and behaviors are all connected. Each one influences the other. Change just one piece of that chain, and it can ripple out to shift the rest. That's powerful, because it means you don't need to change everything at once—you just need to start with one.

Your thoughts and moods won't always line up with your values or your beliefs. Sometimes your mind says one thing while your heart and morals say another. And that's okay—it's part of being human. You may not always be able to control your situations. You may not always be able to control your thoughts or even your emotions. But you can *always* control your behaviors. You can always choose your actions.

So don't waste your energy stressing over what you can't control. Focus on what you can. Let go of the rest and trust that life has a way of working itself out in your favor. And even in hard times—even when things feel heavy—there's growth happening. You don't need to go looking for suffering, but when it shows up, look for the lesson in it. Difficult seasons make the easier ones shine brighter.

Not every thought that runs through your head is true. We're wired to have both positive and negative thoughts, logical and illogical ones, thoughts that help us and thoughts that harm us. The brain was never meant to be perfect—it was meant to be human. That's why you can't take every thought seriously.

Instead, practice ignoring certain thoughts. Starve them of your attention. Some thoughts can be restructured—flipped into something more positive—but others are best left alone. Sometimes trying to fight a thought just feeds it more energy, and it lingers. Like a fire, some things die out quicker if you stop giving them oxygen.

Fill your mind with mantras, images, or distractions that actually serve you. Shift your focus toward what uplifts you, not what drags you down. When you're in a negative mood, notice how your thoughts automatically turn negative too. All of a sudden, what used to be great seems terrible. But those thoughts aren't the truth—they're just temporary reflections of your state of mind.

It's okay to feel emotions of every kind—joy, sadness, anger, fear, frustration. That's part of our humanity. And remember this: emotions pass. Even the heavy ones. They come, they peak, and then they move on if you let them. The problem is when we cling to them. A lot of negativity lingers simply because we won't release it.

When you do feel negative emotions, the healthiest thing you can do is **cope and express them in ways that heal instead of harm.** Journaling, talking to someone you trust, reading, praying, communicating your exact feelings, or distracting yourself with an activity you enjoy—these are outlets that can actually make you feel better almost immediately. On the other hand, unhealthy outlets—lashing out, bottling up, self-destructive habits—can make the situation worse and drag you deeper.

Also, remember: not everything your mind says is a big deal. You don't need to take every thought or feeling so seriously. Learn to dismiss what doesn't serve you. Ignore it. Pay less attention to it. That's strength too.

And if you need help, ask for it. There's nothing weak about seeking guidance or support. Receiving can be just as important as giving.

Finally, be clear about what you want from life. Write down your values, your priorities, your goals—short-term and long-term. Journal your plans, your steps, your visions. That clarity helps you manage your thoughts and emotions because it gives you direction. It reminds you of where you're headed.

Frequently remember it's ok don't be a victim of inevitable imperfections of life be a survivor, a thriver, Practice acceptance, apply mindfulness use awareness and observe with non judgmental lens. You don't have to change your thoughts, your feelings, your situation, your physical sensations, just shift the angle in which you perceive, see it differently,

14

make peace with your imperfections, make peace with your thoughts, feelings, situation and physical sensations by making peace I mean just acknowledging that it's ok, it's normal, it happens, it's life, you can still make change from a peaceful place, make peace with life's imperfections, we all go through the life motions it's ok. It's not your obligation to control everything, it's not your obligation to change the world, people, or even yourself. Just let a lot of humanity and life just be, even if you tried there's a lot of life that you can't control or change. It's ok though just do what you can and acknowledge your limitations, also acknowledge and be accepting of life and humanity imperfections. Allow yourself to see the bigger picture of life and humanity, don't get consumed by the small imperfect parts, see the whole image, the abundance/plentiness of beauty in it too.

Life becomes easier to navigate when you learn this balance: control what you can, let go of what you can't, and express yourself in ways that free you instead of trap you.

Chapter 7: Get Out of Your Head

Alot of times, we just need to get out of our heads. You don't have to live in your mind all the time. Be present. Be in your life. Overthinking can pull you away from reality, distract you, keep you stuck, or stop you from enjoying what's right in front of you.

Your brain is a tool, not a prison. Use it when you need to—when you're solving problems, creating, planning, or reflecting—but don't live trapped inside it. Not every moment needs to be analyzed. Not every situation needs to be replayed or broken down. Sometimes the best thing you can do is simply step out of your thoughts and step into your life.

Don't think about it too much. Don't dive so deep that you drown in your own thoughts. Thinking too much can create confusion, negativity, and even paralyze you from taking action. The truth is, clarity often comes after movement, not before it.

So next time you feel yourself overthinking, try moderation. Think enough to point yourself in the right direction, then move. Take a step—any step. Even the smallest steps will carry you far over time. Action builds momentum, and momentum builds confidence.

You don't have to have it all figured out right now. It's okay not to know everything. Life unfolds step by step, and often you'll only see the answers once you've already started moving. Have faith in that.

Take leaps of faith: faith in yourself, faith in people, faith in God. Believe that God will provide you with exactly what you need, exactly when you need it. Life has a way of aligning when you trust it.

Be courageous. Be honorable. Be yourself. Life will adjust around the real you, not the masked or fearful version of you. Refuse to limit yourself because of fear or because of what others might think. Don't clip your own wings just to fit in someone else's box.

Fly how you want to fly. Reach for what you want to reach. Live boldly, not trapped in your head, but free in your life.

Chapter 8: Courage and Taking Action Despite Any Feeling

We've all been there. There's something we really want to do—something we know will move us forward—but our feelings get in the way. Maybe we don't feel like it. Maybe the weight of our emotions makes it hard to push through. And so we stall. We freeze. We let those feelings hold us back from the action we truly want to take.

Here's the truth: you won't always be able to control your feelings. You won't always be able to control your thoughts either. That's life. But you *can* always control your actions. That's where your power lives.

Don't waste your energy focusing on what's outside your control. Focus on what you can do—your choices, your behavior, your next step. That's all it takes: one step.

Sometimes that step means leaving your comfort zone. And yes, stepping outside of what feels familiar can be uncomfortable. But it's also where growth begins. Every time you act with courage despite fear, despite resistance, despite not "feeling like it," you build a new kind of pride in yourself. You realize how strong you are. You see yourself becoming the kind of person who doesn't bow to fear.

Taking action shifts everything. When you change your behavior, your thoughts and feelings often follow. Suddenly, what once felt impossible becomes possible. The situation looks brighter, your confidence grows, and your emotions begin to align with your actions.

So choose courage. Choose to act despite fear, despite doubt, despite discomfort. Choose to step forward even when your feelings try to hold you back.

At the end of the day, you are the master of yourself. Your feelings are not your master. Your thoughts are not your master. You hold the key.

Courage is not the absence of fear—it's moving forward in spite of it. That's real strength. That's freedom. Embrace uncertainty with hopefulness, courage and confidence in that we shall welcome an unexplained magic to our lives. In that we achieve plenty and even that in which we didn't even expect. So, go after that which you desire, enjoy the journey, the process, the steps and succeed in attaining your desires.

Chapter 9: Openness

Be open. Open to understanding others' perspectives, philosophies, beliefs, opinions, and feelings. Be open to trying new things, learning new things, adventuring, meeting new people, going to new places, tasting different foods. Be open to new hobbies, new routines, breaking cycles and habits.

Be open to a better future, a better now, a more improved life. Be open to making a difference, to creating a positive impact, to living a more meaningful life. Be open to acquiring a greater, deeper, more profound way of living.

Be open to stepping outside your comfort zone and pushing past your feelings. Be open to shifting if you really want to. Be open to being graceful and loving—even when you feel like someone doesn't deserve it.

Stay open-minded. There will be moments when your thoughts and feelings push you to close off, but be open to the possibility of change with time. Open your heart to love and show love not only to your friends and family, but to the world as a whole.

Be open-hearted.

Chapter 10: Don't Sweat It #Stress

I can't stress this enough—don't freakin' sweat it. We often stress about small stuff, simple stuff, big stuff a bit too much. Here's the thing: when stress pops up, use it as a tool and dismiss it. Usually stress is reminding us of things we need to do, but we somehow almost always overindulge in it. Just use it as a reminder and kick it to the curb. Don't prepare for the worst—prepare for the best and put that into existence. A wise friend named Chris H once told me, *"Ask yourself, is there something you can do about it right now? If yes, then why stress about it? If not, then why stress about it?"* Such simple but one of the greatest pieces of advice I've heard. Also, when we stress we tend to make things much bigger than they are.

There's also other stresses that pop up: mistakes, mistakes you possibly made, mistakes you might make. Beating yourself up about mistakes isn't helping you or anybody—just learn from your mistake and move on. It may be difficult, but with time and effort, anything is possible. For stressing about mistakes you might make, figure out solutions on how to get what you want, prepare to get what you want. You can always control your actions—take actions on getting what you want, not avoiding what you don't want. Put your focus on what you want, not preparing defenses. Have faith in yourself and the higher powers that when the time comes, you'll be able to gear yourself towards what's best or right for you.

Last but not least: irrational stress and worries. I want you to recognize these stresses and worries as what they are—irrational. Label them as irrationality, then dismiss those thoughts. You can ignore or distract yourself with something else, or think about something positive. Positive thoughts are 100x more powerful than negative thoughts.

Avoid wallowing in stress and negativity. Let that time or moment work itself out when it comes. Have faith you'll work it out when it comes. Have faith in your inner wisdom and guidance. Have faith in the higher powers. It's vital for your overall wellbeing to make the most out of the present moment. Enjoy and appreciate the present moment because it truly is a present.

We often rush and try to get things done like it's an emergency, like it's life or death, which can cause stress and hostile feelings. Let's constantly remind ourselves that it's not an emergency—it's not life or death. We dedicate our lives to getting things done like it's an emergency, and we forget that life's purpose isn't about getting all of it done, but to live a life filled with love and joy.

Some funny things that can trigger stress and hostility are rushing, moving like it's an emergency, thinking too much or too deep, taking it too seriously, being too hard or too strict, not using your understanding, and being critically judgmental. So ease up—it's not that serious, it's not that deep. Think moderately. Be more understanding and less judgmental. Always remind yourself it's ok.

Have faith in yourself, in people, in higher powers. Like MLK said, you don't have to see the whole staircase—just take the leap of faith, take the step, have faith it'll work out, it'll be well. I highly recommend a book called *Don't Sweat the Small Stuff… and It's All Small Stuff* by Richard Carlson. It's a lovely self-help book that has solutions to a lot of our day-to-day challenges and, of course, it's definitely helpful for managing stress.

Chapter 11: Don't let the past or future steal your present

Seize the present moment and enjoy it to your best ability, if we never enjoy our present then when are we ever gonna enjoy it? We spend our present wallowing in the past or worrying about the future sometimes. Let's not do that, it's that simple decisions are the doorway to destiny and everything. Let's enjoy our present moments cause the only moment we have is the nows, the present moments, if we spend all of our present moments in the past or future when are we ever gonna enjoy the present. Feel free to learn from your mistakes, reminisce about a good time, plan and prepare for the future moderately other than that stay in the present yes it can be a little difficult sometimes but there's no challenge we can't conquer within, so don't feed into those tendencies to wallow in the past or worry about the future, let the future worry about itself and let the past be in the past, Don't worry about the future or tomorrow you have enough to enjoy and work on today the future and tomorrow belongs to the the higher powers have faith you'll be well provided for. Seize the moments and opportunities, reap the beautiful abundant benefits of being in the present moment. Don't ever underestimate the power and benefits of the present on what it can do for you and the impact it has on the world around you.

Make time each day to reflect, our need for reflection sometimes can distract us from our present moment, or disturb your peace of mind. Reflecting can help you better understand yourself, your needs, wants and plans. Also reflect moderately, don't think too much. Don't think too deeply into anything, and don't feed into all your thoughts, positive or negative, let some thoughts just pass. Keep it simple, don't put too much weight on your shoulders, relax, enjoy life. It shall come whatever you please. It's just a matter of time and keep your faith and hopefulness in it.

Chapter 12: Spirituality

Please please please don't condemn people for their spiritual or religious beliefs. God don't want us condemning each other—He wants us to love each other and be accepting of each other. Nobody wants to be condemned, so why do it? We all wanna be accepted, loved, and supported. Love people to have their own path just as you like to have your own. We all have that ego that wants to condemn people and make ourselves believe that we're better—let's not feed into that. Choose being humble, kind, loving, accepting, understanding, and open-hearted, feed into that.

There's many right paths in life—it's just really about what's right for you. We were all created uniquely; can't expect everybody to be into the same ideas and roads. Just because something is right for you doesn't mean it'll be right for somebody else. What floats my boat may not float your boat—that's life. We're all unique in our own ways. There are many elegant paths—religious, spiritual, etc.—for a reason, and many good people that follow each different one. It's just whatever floats your boat, what's right for what brings you bliss. Live your life how you wanna live it. Nobody should have to feel they are being condemned for their beliefs—we all deserve to be accepted and supported, no matter what path we choose or our differences. God is the most loving, merciful, gracious, beneficent, accepting, and graceful there is.

Keep a balance with spirituality or religiousness. Don't be too hard or too strict on yourself, especially when it's taking a toll on your overall wellbeing and happiness. Do things for the higher power, but also do things for yourself or people. It's ok to make time for fun, for joy. It's ok to break a few religious or spiritual rules as long as you're not really hurting anybody or yourself. Enjoy what life has to offer. There's nowhere in the sky that says you're supposed to live a certain way—just do what brings you happiness and be accepting and graceful of people and your humanity. God doesn't want us to be too hard or too strict—He wants us to be happy and enjoy life. Follow what makes you happy, and an abundance of good things will follow.

God created us to be human, and each of us uniquely, so He expects us to be human and be our unique selves. Choose our own uniquely "cocktailed" paths for our specific bliss. God doesn't want us to be perfectionists—He knows that takes a toll on our happiness or living a way someone else is expecting. Live any which way or how you wanna live. Trust your instincts, have the courage to be yourself, and choose your own path that brings you bliss. Best believe the most loving, compassionate, and gracious wants you as happy as can be. Choose the path that brings you the most bliss, and don't settle for anything less than the path you desire and are naturally attracted to the most. Have faith. Believe an abundance of good things will follow, for following your bliss.

Chapter 13: Choose to Focus More on the Good

There's both good and bad to focus on—positive or negative, what you want or what you don't want, hopefulness or hopelessness, weakness or strength—it's your choice. If you wanna welcome happiness, you gotta choose to focus mainly on the good. Focus on what's right, what's good about life, people, yourself—not on flaws, imperfections, or mistakes. Wherever you put your attention, it influences everything. Your perception, your interpretation of life, of people—it shapes your whole experience. A wise therapist named Kayla once shared a quote she learned from photography, "When life gets blurry, adjust your focus." Phenomenal, million-dollar quote right there, real talk.

Enjoy and appreciate the little things, the new things, the challenges, the big things, the people—basically everything good that life puts in front of you. Appreciate what you got. Shift your vocabulary to "I get to." Appreciate your family, friends, and people in general. Everybody matters. Every single person. Yes, even the person at the cash register, the gas station, grocery store, fast food, restaurants, truck drivers, janitors, warehouse workers—you get the point. Life doesn't run without them. We all got roles. We all got value. We all got purpose. "All labor that uplifts humanity has dignity and importance and should be undertaken with painstaking excellence."-MLK. We all have immense value. If you were given life you are meaningful, each of us, all of us.

Be humble. Wish people the best. Stay away from envy, jealousy, resentment. Those things only weigh you down. Wish people well and watch life respond in kind. A positive attitude toward seeing other people enjoy life attracts more of that good energy to you. It's real.

Shoot for the stars. Focus on what can go right. Think about how good it could go, what if it turns out better than you ever imagined? Be optimistic, hopeful, and wishful. Don't feed the doubts, fears, limitations. Don't shrink yourself. Ponder the good. Ponder what brings you joy, not misery. Fill your mind with positivity. Train your brain like a muscle. Thoughts are habits. Negative thoughts will come, they always do, but don't feed them. One positive thought is hundreds of times stronger than a negative thought. Rule your mind. Don't let it rule you.

Be present. Relax. Stay faithful and hopeful about the future. With your subconscious mind working with you, you'll get directed, guided, and things will flow. Good hopeful thinking brings good things. Have faith in yourself, people, the higher powers, and the abundance of good in life.

There's always something you think you're "missing out" on. There's always something. Where are you gonna put your focus? Quit obsessing over what you don't have. Appreciate what you do have. Focus on what you want, sure, but don't frame it as missing out. Understand that life's timing and the paths we take are unique. Certain things are prescribed for your journey. Respect that. Enjoy the journey itself. Don't just chase the finish line. If you only love the end, you'll miss life itself. Fall in love with the process.

Don't give too much attention to the negative parts of humanity—look at the good. There's way more good than bad, way more positive than negative. It all depends on your focus. Focus on good and you'll flow toward good. Good will gravitate toward you. What you focus on influences what you experience, what you attract, and what you create.

Think, Focus, Ponder, Feel, Imagine, Speak, Believe, Assume that which is hopeful, wishful, optimistic, lovely, positive and good. Put energy there. Let it grow. Let it move through you. Let it manifest. Good things will come in ways you don't even expect.

Chapter 14: Faith

Always remember to have faith. We forget sometimes, get caught up in doubts, worries, or overthinking. Remind yourself—have faith in yourself, faith in people, faith in God, faith that good things will happen. Have faith that it will get better. Have faith the hard times will pass. Have faith you'll prosper and succeed. Have faith you are blessed, that your days are blessed, that life itself is blessed.

If trust is hard for you, start small. Try a little faith. A little trust. It will grow if you nurture it. Don't give up on faith. Keep it alive. Have faith it'll work out. Have faith you can handle whatever comes your way. Have faith it'll turn out in your best interest, that life will work in your favor. Have faith you'll be able to see the good in everything and make the most out of what life offers.

Have faith God won't put you in a situation you can't handle. Have faith in your efforts and in God's will. Life doesn't always go the way we plan. We set a path, and sometimes we take detours. It doesn't go exactly how we want it to—but there's a reason. Try to see the good, the silver lining, the benefit in everything. Life sometimes gives detours we don't want, but have faith—they're for your good, even if you can't see it now. Just trust. Just believe. Faith is your compass when everything else feels uncertain.

Chapter 15: Healthy Limits, Prioritizing Mental Health

Prioritize healthy limits. We all have boundaries for what we can handle and what keeps us happy. Sometimes we exceed those limits, and of course, it takes a toll on our well-being. Even if it's temporary, many times it's just not worth it. Nothing is worth risking your happiness or peace of mind. Prioritize your happiness and overall well-being. If something is going to take too much out of you, simply don't do it. If you feel like enough is enough, and any more will negatively affect your well-being, then end it for now. Do something else that brings you joy. That alone welcomes balance, peace, and a healthier state of being.

Do what's best for you, your happiness, and your overall well-being, while still being considerate of others. Keep balance. I'm not saying always do what you feel like doing—your feelings don't always align with your values, nor do they always lead you toward what's best or what welcomes happiness. Make sure logic is in the picture when acting on impulse or desire. Maintain healthy limits. It's essential.

A wise man named Marquan once told me: *"People use the term 'people pleaser' in a negative connotation. There's nothing wrong with being a people pleaser as long as you keep it at a healthy level, a healthy limit."* That stuck with me and helped me see the importance of balance in all aspects. Kindness, helping others, people-pleasing, and even trying to please God—these are all good things, but they need to exist at healthy levels. Be responsible with your possessions, your energy, and your overall well-being. If you try to be everything to be everybody you'll end up being nothing to nobody including yourself. If you try to be everywhere at the same time you'll end up nowhere, don't spread yourself too thin. Prioritise a life filled with quality and peace of mind.

Sometimes we get so caught up in what's outside of us that we forget the importance of taking care of our mental health. We overindulge even when we know moderation is healthier for our overall well-being. We make excuses for why we can't be happy, improve, or get better—but in reality, we're just holding ourselves back and feeding into the negative parts of our humanity.

It's okay to need help. Sometimes I need help with my mental health, so I speak with a professional. Great therapy sessions are incredibly helpful. There is absolutely nothing wrong with seeking professional guidance— it's genius, if you ask me. It shows you're prioritizing your mental health and well-being. Your mind is the main place you function from; taking care of it is honorable and essential.

Think of it like this: if your car is broken and you can't fix it yourself, you take it to a professional. Why not do the same for your mind when it needs help? Self-help/psychology books, like *Mind Over Mood Christine A.*

Padesky, PhD and Dennis Greenberger, PhD. , can also be excellent tools for therapy, improving mental health and coping. You can always improve your mental health and overall well-being. You just need to put in the effort and believe in yourself.

Seeking help and having faith is half the job. The other half is putting in the work. Apply yourself consistently. Believe it, practice it, put in the work, and you can achieve it. Take care of your mental health and well-being—it's worth it. You are worth it.

Chapter 16: Balance

If you lose balance in your life, you lose and miss out on a lot of the good things that are essential for your well-being. Balance is vital—for your happiness, your mental health, your sense of peace, and your overall life satisfaction. Keep everything at healthy levels. You will naturally know what is taking a negative toll on you.

Keep work, career, school, helping others, people-pleasing, God-pleasing, and self-pleasures at healthy levels. Maintain limits. Be moderate in whatever you do in life. That is the key to maintaining balance. We all have an innate understanding of what moderation looks like for ourselves. We know when we're overwhelmed or overextending ourselves. Don't be too hard on yourself, but don't be too easy either. Don't be overly strict with yourself, with others, or with religion and spirituality. Don't take everything too seriously. Ease up, relax.

Don't spend all of your life just on work or career. Make time for family, friends, adventure, hobbies, fun, and relaxation. I've seen it in others and experienced it myself—people often focus too heavily on one area of life. They become too strict, too hard, overly invested or overly indulgent in one thing, whether it's work, school, religion, or spirituality. This causes them to lose balance. They forget, disregard, or procrastinate making time for the other amazing things in life—spending time with loved ones, hanging out, having fun, self-care, resting, hobbies, and exercising.

We must maintain a healthy rhythm in life. A good balance comes from recognizing all the areas that make life rich and meaningful—and giving each its due attention. Life is not a surgery operation or an emergency. Too often we approach it as if it's one, being too strict, too hard, too serious, or overly indulgent in one area. In doing so, we overlook the amazing fruits God created for us—the simple joys, the relationships, the moments of peace, love, and adventure. We forget to make time for the other beautiful things life has to offer. Balance is the key to experiencing all of it fully.

Chapter 17: Love and Self-Love

Love is in the air. Love is in the world. Love is in the universe. Love resides within each and every one of us. Unleash it. Release it. Love yourself. Love the people around you. Love the food, the things in life. Love the animals, love the plants. Love and appreciate your blessings and everything you have.

Love for other people's success and happiness, just as you would wish it for yourself. Show your love. Express your love. Don't be shy. Love is an amazing force—push past that shyness. You can do it. Wishing people the best is expressing love for them.

We can't choose to be flawless, to be without weaknesses or imperfections. But we can see the innocence in everybody. See the good in everyone because it exists in all of us. Express that love within yourself. Say it in your heart: *"I wish that person the best,"* even if you don't like what they do or have done. Still, see the good, the innocence, the potential.

If we all had the choice, we would likely all choose perfection. But love yourself as you are. Love and appreciate all the things you like about yourself. Love the way the higher power created you. Be grateful for it, but also be graceful with yourself. Be comfortable with your imperfections, with your humanity. None of us are perfect—we all have flaws.

God created us to be beautiful, elegant, and unique. He also created us to be human, which comes with flaws. That's the balance. That's life. We are all beautiful, all special, all capable of expressing love. Yes, we have opinions, we make mistakes, and that's okay. It is part of our humanity. But remember the greater truth: we were created by the greatest.

Chapter 18: See the Good in Everything

That's the gist of it—see the good in everything. Not that everything is good, but that you put forth the effort to see the silver lining. See the benefit, the opportunity, the love in situations, even if it's hard. Even when it's difficult, have faith that there is something good in it.

They say everything happens for a reason. And that's true—just have faith. Even a little faith is enough, as long as you're trying. Belief is powerful—more powerful than you realize.

See your problems as teachers. See difficulties as opportunities for growth. See the chance to improve, to practice patience, grace, acceptance, gratitude, and love. See the chance to practice managing your thoughts and emotions, coping in healthy ways, being understanding, and giving the benefit of the doubt.

See the good in your challenges. Have faith that it's all for the good, even if you don't understand it yet. Keep looking, keep trying, keep believing—the good is always there if you're willing to see it.

Chapter 19: Human Interacting and Socializing

We are social creatures. Humans are meant to socialize and interact with other humans. We need connection—real interaction—or we start to feel the negative consequences of isolation. Human interaction is part of our nature. It fulfills needs we can't ignore.

You'll learn to know how much interaction is enough for you. That's why they say not to isolate. Constant isolation takes a toll on your mind, your emotions, your energy—it goes against human nature. Some of the greatest days in life involve people. Don't miss out. Make time to hang out, to talk, to laugh, to share moments with others.

Value socializing and interacting—it's important. Love the people around you. Even if you don't click with everyone, there are plenty of people you are deeply compatible with. We all share this thing called humanity, and when you connect with the right people, it's magic. Trust that there are so many people out there you're compatible with—more than you could ever meet or hang out with. There is an abundance waiting for your needs, just seek it and you'll find it.

Let this serve as extra motivation: make time to hang out with friends, family, and people in general. Interaction isn't just for you—it's a benefit for them too. Never underestimate the value of your presence, the company you bring, and the energy you share. Connection is abundant. All good things in life are abundant.

Chapter 20: Be a Survivor, Not a Victim

The way you tell the story—your story—to yourself and to others matters. The words you choose, the tone you use, the way you explain it—all of that influences whether your story is a survivor story or a victim story. You have the choice.

Speaking to yourself and to people in a victim-like way or tonality can shape your mindset in an unhealthy manner. It can lead to negative thoughts, negative feelings, limiting beliefs. It can hold you back from reaching your potential and can even push people away. Life becomes heavier when you see yourself as a victim. Be a survivor and put forth the effort to thrive and reach for all you desire. You are the shaper of your life.

Instead, adopt the mindset of a survivor. Believe that whatever you went through didn't break you mentally, emotionally, or spiritually. Believe it made you stronger, smarter, wiser, and a better version of yourself. Tough times are teachers—they build resilience, courage, and clarity.

Life is often experienced the way you believe it will be. So believe you are a survivor. Feel the power, the strength, and the confidence that comes with that mindset. Speak about your experiences as a survivor, not as a victim. The lens through which you view your life shapes your reality.

Don't live in a "why me" mindset. Live in a "try me" mindset. Believe in your ability to handle whatever comes your way—wisely, strategically, and with strength. You are what you believe. Your life is what you make it through your beliefs. Choose survival, choose growth, choose power.

Chapter 21: Accountability and Blaming

When we are unhappy, what do we do? We blame. When things go wrong, when life doesn't go exactly the way we wanted, when mistakes happen, we blame. Blaming can make you feel powerless. Taking accountability makes you feel powerful—powerful over your life, your happiness, and yourself.

It's not a good idea to base your happiness on how others treat you or what they do. That's outside of your control. Take responsibility for your own happiness. Don't blame others for the way you feel. The power to feel joy, peace, or contentment is entirely within you. Next time you feel upset or unhappy, blame your humanity if you must—but then take charge. Make yourself happy again. You can. Life becomes much easier, lighter, and more enjoyable when you take responsibility for your emotions instead of pointing fingers.

Accountability isn't always easy. None of us like being wrong, flawed, or imperfect. Our ego fights it—it wants to blame others to avoid admitting our own weaknesses. But yes, people behave in ways we don't prefer. That's life. And guess what? It's all up to you what you do with your feelings about it. You create the feeling, even if you didn't want it. Our humanity is imperfect; life won't always go our way. That's the point. Embrace accountability—it makes you feel grounded, in control, and strong.

Chapter 22: Sleep

Sleep is vital. No, scratch that—it's essential. For every single part of your life, sleep matters. Make time for it. Without enough good sleep, you're risking more than just feeling tired. Your peace suffers. Your happiness dips. Your focus, intellect, and patience waver. Your body and health pay the price. Everything is affected when you skimp on sleep.

Don't perceive sleeping as a waste of time or down time where no progress is occurring. You'd be surprised what the back room of your mind is doing while you are asleep. The subconscious part of your mind doesn't sleep in terms of progressing and prospering. It's actually cooking up some good thangs for your present and future whilst awake or asleep, the power of the back room of your mind is phenomenal. It's nurturing and growing the seeds you've sown in your mind the beliefs, the assumptions, the imaginations, the desires, the plans, the goals, and the ideas we hold soo dearly. Sleep also increases your healing and rejuvenation properties, which leads to an effect of maximizing your quality in life, in everything.

Value it. Protect it. Prioritize it. Make it non-negotiable. When you care for your sleep, you care for your overall well-being. You maximize the positive effect it has on yourself, on your relationships, and even on the world around you. Good sleep welcomes clarity, calm, and happiness. It helps you show up as your best self, ready to handle life, tackle challenges, and enjoy the moments you have. Don't underestimate it. Sleep isn't optional—it's foundational.

Chapter 23: Grace

We all receive God's grace. His kindness, mercy, love, acceptance, and help—sometimes even when we don't deserve it. That's the beauty of grace. Sometimes it comes as tough love, but even that is for our good.

We also carry that grace within us. Created in God's image, we inherit fragments of His goodness, love, and compassion—not to His degree, obviously, but it's still there. Have faith in it. Have faith in God's grace. Know that He will always love you, no matter what, and always accept you exactly as you are, flaws and mistakes included. You are human. You were created imperfect by design.

When you mess up, see it as a small part of the bigger picture—part of our shared humanity. Give yourself grace. Practice self-compassion. Treat yourself with kindness, understanding, and acceptance. Forgive yourself, even if it feels undeserved—you do deserve it. You're human. Imperfect. Flawed. And that's okay. Wallowing in the negative doesn't help anyone. Move forward. Learn. Grow.

Having even a little grace creates and shows tremendous strength in handling your feelings also in managing your imperfections, it's very powerful, it sure will welcome good tidings. Assume the best intentions, try your best, practice it, it's very healthy, it welcomes happiness and breeds good in your life, restrain yourself from negative judgments. Extend grace to others too. Even when someone wrongs you, practice forgiveness, patience, and understanding. Everyone has their own challenges, limitations, and flaws. You don't need to be friends with everyone—but you can show them grace. Help when you can, be kind even when it's hard, and practice empathy. Just remember: healthy limits and boundaries matter too. Grace isn't about losing yourself—it's about lifting yourself also others while staying true and being healthy to your own well-being.

Chapter 24: Be Humble

Humbleness is one of the greatest keys to peace of mind. Condemning others does no good for you, only harm. Don't let the ego trick you into looking down on people or trying to prove you're above them. Arrogance is a trap—it brings insecurity, constant comparison, and the endless chase for outside validation, reassurance, and approval. When you walk in arrogance, you set yourself up to always prove you're better, nitpick flaws, and search for faults in others. That mindset blinds you from seeing the good in people, because you're too busy measuring yourself against them.

So here's the truth: let go of arrogance. Drop it. You don't need it. Instead, try to live with the mindset that we are all equal. Yes, we all have different challenges, flaws, strengths, weaknesses, blessings, and desires. We hold different views, beliefs, and mistakes. But underneath it all, we share one thing in common: our humanity. Everything you have is only possible because of the higher power. Without that higher power, none of it exists. Just as easily he gives to you he can easily give to anybody, recognize we all have great potential.

So remember—just because somebody is different doesn't mean they are less. The person who works at the gas station, the warehouse, the grocery store—every role matters, every person matters. We all have our purposes, our value, and our place in this world.

Instead of comparing yourself to people, compare yourself to your past self. That's the only competition worth running. Work on being a better version of you, not on being "better" than somebody else. Be grateful for what you have, learn to see the good in people, and never belittle anyone. Wish everybody the best. Love openly, without arrogance.

There is more than enough for all of us to enjoy and have. Life is beautifully abundant. Good things exist in endless supply. Humility opens the door for you to enjoy that abundance fully, and to share it freely with others.

Chapter 25: Self Validation

Nothing to prove, baby. Self-validated, self-confident, secure within myself. I've got nothing to prove to anybody but myself. That's freedom. That's peace. That's strength.

See, here's the thing—if you don't believe in yourself, how can you expect anyone else to? If you're walking around waiting on somebody else to crown you, to give you permission, to clap for you, to call you worthy—you'll be waiting forever. Because the main validation, the real approval, the solid reassurance—the one that sticks and holds you together when nobody's around—has to come from *within*.

Somewhere along the line, we slipped. We started putting too much weight on other people's opinions. We started checking for their applause, their nods, their likes, their follows, their comments. We started feeding ourselves on "outside validation" like it was the main meal. But outside validation? That's just appetizers. Tastes good for a second, but it's not enough to fill you. The real nourishment, the main course—the kind that actually satisfies and sustains—comes only from within yourself.

So reassure yourself. Approve yourself. Love yourself. Talk to yourself the way you wish others would talk to you. Tell yourself the truth even when your feelings try to lie. Stand in your own corner. Be your own cheerleader. Be your own supporter. Because here's the truth: what people think of you doesn't matter as much as you think. What *you* think of you— that's what really matters. It's ok to care what others think of you just make sure it exists at a healthy level, a healthy limit, not to a point where you are constantly stressed about it or super self conscious or you are being self destructive or it's depleting your mental health or it's affecting you being your true self. A healthy level where you are considerate or thoughtful of others in terms of being compassionate now that's a healthy manner.

Quit wasting time worrying about what others might say or might think, because honestly, most people aren't paying attention to you like you imagine. People are caught up in their own storms, their own insecurities, their own lives. They're trying to survive, too. So don't let imaginary judgment stop you. Don't hand over your peace to people who aren't even thinking about you like that.

Validate yourself. Give yourself what you've been waiting for others to give. Accept and believe the ideas you want to be validated on. Live them. Speak them into yourself. Stand firm in them. Because you are what you believe you are, and your life unfolds through the lens of your beliefs. What you believe will happen, will come to pass. So why not choose to believe in greatness? Why not choose to believe in favor, abundance, growth, love, success?

Start declaring it. Write it. Feel it. Repeat it. Let it sink into your spirit:

- I am beautiful.

- I am prospering

- I am loved.

- I am wanted.

- I am attractive.

- I am enough.

- I am smart.

- I am amazing.

- I am kind.

- I am making a positive impact.

- I dress amazingly.

- I am succeeding and progressing.

- I have a great work ethic.

- I am successful.

- I am okay just the way I am.

Believe it. Feel it. Own it. Validation starts from within--and once it does, the feelings of confidence will come pouring in and it'll also radiate from you to others. That's the kind of self-validation that builds you from the inside out. That's the foundation nobody can shake.

Let these truths be your foundation. Say them until they feel natural. Say them until they don't feel like words anymore, but reality. Because once you truly validate yourself, once you become secure within, nobody can strip that from you. Not rejection. Not criticism. Not silence. Not the lack of likes or followers or claps. Your worth won't be moved, because your worth won't be tied to them—it'll be tied to you.

Self-validation is freedom. It's waking up and realizing you don't have to prove anything. You don't have to compete with people. You don't have to beg for approval. You don't have to perform to be worthy. You already are.

And when you really feel that, when you live from that place? That's when life changes. That's when you walk lighter. That's when you can show up fully as yourself without fear. That's when confidence stops being something you chase and starts being something you carry.

So go ahead. Take your power back. Be the one who tells yourself, *"I am enough."*

Chapter 26 — Hope and Manifestation

Hope is oxygen for the soul. I once heard on a commercial, "hope is the anchor to our souls." Without it, we suffocate in despair. With it, we can survive anything. When you hold on to hope, you give yourself the strength to keep moving even when the road feels endless, even when the night feels too long. Hope is the quiet whisper that says, *"Keep going, there's something better on the other side."*

Here's the key—highly expect, but don't demand. Expect good things shall come to pass. Expect blessings, opportunities, breakthroughs, and healings. But don't cling to it with a rigid, 100% demand, because life is unpredictable. Sometimes it shows up differently than you imagined. Sometimes it comes later than you planned. Sometimes it comes disguised as struggle first. That doesn't mean it won't happen—it means the Higher Power is working it out in the way that's best for you. An honorable therapist Laura H mentioned "have faith in your effort, you can't force anybody to do anything", true that, trying to force or trying too hard for things to happen, well we all know what that brings about. It's always better and healthier to relax, to put in effort that suffices, not too much.

Have faith it shall be divinely constructed or put together for it to unfold in our presence, stay hopeful, stay optimistic.

Believe that it will get better. Believe that no difficulty is forever. Everything passes eventually—the storms, the heartbreak, the setbacks, the pain. Nothing stays the same. Seasons shift. Life moves. And through it all, the Higher Power knows what's good for you, what's best for you, what will shape you. It's all for a reason. Even if you don't see the reason right now, trust that it's part of something bigger, something greater.

Never give up hope. Because hope breeds resilience. Hope is the fuel that carries you through your hardest battles. Hope is the rope you cling to when you feel like you're drowning. And even when you don't feel like holding on, hold on anyway. Because blessings are on the way. The story is not finished.

Now let's talk about manifestation. What you believe, what you accept, what you assume—it usually comes to pass. Good or bad. Your subconscious mind is like fertile soil—it doesn't care what you plant. It just grows what you put in it. If you plant fear, doubt, negativity, you'll see it sprout in your life in events, conditions, relationships, experiences. If you plant faith, positivity, elegance, luxury, beauty, confidence, joy, you'll watch it bloom into blessings and opportunities. So be careful what you believe. Be intentional about what you accept. Choose wisely what you allow to take root in your mind.

Manifestation is not about forcing things—it's about aligning yourself with what you already believe is yours. Speak it. Feel it. Walk as if you already possess it. Pray for it, then believe it's already on the way. That's faith. That's power. That's hope in action.

And listen, I highly recommend you read *The Power of Your Subconscious Mind* if you want to go deeper into this. That book will show you how powerful your mind really is, how your thoughts and beliefs shape your entire reality.

Be hopeful of yourself. Be hopeful of people. Be hopeful of life. Believe that good is here in abundance. Because the truth is—there is an overflow of blessings, opportunities, and love in this world. The ones who see it, receive it. The ones who believe it, live it. Abundance is always available, but it reveals itself to those who expect it and who believe it there for us all.

So keep your heart open. Keep your faith alive. Keep your hope strong. Manifest wisely. And never forget—what you carry in your mind, you will eventually carry in your hands, it shall come to pass in your experience.

Chapter 27: Gratitude

It's okay to want more, but don't make your happiness contingent on it. Focus less on what you want and more on what you already have. Your happiness is not determined by what you possess—it's determined by how you think and perceive what you already have.

Appreciate everything. Especially the little things—our lives are full of countless small blessings. Appreciate every little step, every small progress. Seek progress can't be mad at making progress, not perfection, seeking perfection and not achieving it because imperfection is bound to happen, it's inevitable, leads to a lot of frustrations.. Life wasn't meant to be perfect, and neither are humans. Slip-ups will happen; that's natural. Progress matters. Perfectionism only holds you back. Once a week for 5 minutes write down what you are grateful for and experience the magic it welcomes in your life.

You will never be fully satisfied, and that's okay. Knowing this prevents constant frustration and endless chasing. Satisfaction comes from seeing the cup half full, not half empty. Focus on the good, see the silver lining in every situation—even the challenges. Have faith that the good exists, even if it's hard to see.

Be grateful daily. Instead of thinking about what you don't have, focus on what you do. Instead of dwelling on someone's negative actions, remember the kind or loving actions they've done. Instead of thinking about people you don't like or don't get along with, focus on people you do love and appreciate.

Be grateful for challenges—they teach us patience, resilience, understanding, and growth. See the silver lining. Appreciate the people in your life: family, friends, peers, coworkers, and even the people doing jobs that support society. Everyone has a purpose. Everyone is needed. Your life has meaning as long as you are alive.

Appreciate life, people, and every little blessing—it all matters.

Chapter 28: Choose Wisely What You Engage In

There are endless opportunities to engage in all kinds of things. Millions of things demand your focus, your energy, your attention. Choose wisely what you give yourself to. I'm not saying overthink it—no paralysis by analysis—but yes, trust yourself to quickly recognize what is best, wise, right, and good for you to engage in, and what isn't.

For the most part, mind your own business. We spend too much time and energy on other people's lives. You don't need to step in when someone else is already helping. You don't need to connect people, fix them, or make them do things your way. Most of the time, just let them be. You don't have to know what others are thinking or talking about.

When you focus on your own business, you start creating quality time for the things that truly matter to you, you'll be surprised, the things that actually genuinely benefit your life. When people behave in ways you don't prefer, you don't have to react. Often, silence or walking away is the wisest choice. If you do respond, do so calmly, gracefully, with understanding. You don't have to match someone else's energy—maintain yours. Don't allow other people's behavior to drag you down, upset you, or pull you out of character.

Some engagements can affect your peace. Be conscious of what you let yourself engage in. Protect your energy, protect your mind, protect your happiness. Choose wisely.

Chapter 29: Be Yourself—Come As You Are

You feel best when you're being yourself. It's simple, yet so easy to overcomplicate. Why pretend to be something you're not? Why be a fraud? Not being yourself creates insecurities, stress, and negative feelings. Don't be afraid to fully embrace who you are. Imperfections are part of our humanity—freely being yourself is comforting, freeing, and it truly welcomes happiness.

You don't need to spend time with people who don't accept or love you as you are. Seek those who appreciate you, who accept you, and allow you to fully be yourself. God accepts you exactly as you are, no matter the path you've taken or mistakes you've made. He loves you unconditionally, bestows grace upon you, and created you with the utmost care and purpose.

There are also plenty of people in this world who will love, accept, and appreciate you just as you are. Keep seeking them. Keep seeking the good things in life. Believe that good things are coming and already exist in abundance. Hold that belief, nurture it, and align your life to receive it.

Be you. Truly, unapologetically, wholeheartedly. Happiness comes when you do.

Chapter 30: You Do You, Let People Be

Let people have their own views, beliefs, and perspectives. Let people do them. Let people be right for the sake of kindness and your own peace of mind. Most of the time, you don't need to prove them wrong or waste your energy showing them where they slipped. A lot of situations don't require your time, attention, or energy at all—so let them be.

I'm not saying allow people to walk all over you. I'm saying, for the most part, it's healthier to step back and let others be human. People will always have different flaws, weaknesses, and mistakes than you. Not everyone's imperfections look the same. We were all created uniquely.

Wish them well instead of tearing them down. Try to be as understanding as you can. Try not to take everything so personally or rush into negative judgments. Most of the time, people are doing the best they can with what they know. Some don't know any better. Some haven't yet accepted that there's a better way. Some never learned healthy self-management—whether in emotions, coping skills, or people skills. Some grew up in toxic environments and only repeated what they saw from those they looked up to. Some are still stuck in the same patterns that belonged to the child they once were.

And sometimes people just have bad habits they don't believe they can break, so they justify them instead. That doesn't make them evil—it makes them human. We are all flawed differently. We all make mistakes of different shapes and sizes.

So don't condemn or hold bitterness against someone just because their flaws don't look like yours. If they don't know better today, one day they will. Growth eventually comes, and when it does, they'll look back and realize they were wrong.

Don't forget—we didn't choose to be imperfect. Humanity was designed with flaws stitched right into it. That's part of what makes us human. And because of that, it's better to wish people the best, hope for their growth, and keep your peace instead of letting their mistakes ruin your spirit.

You do you. Let people be. Live your truth, and let them live theirs.

Take responsibility for yourself, and wish the best for everyone else. Accept our shared humanity and know that nobody chose to be imperfect—so extend understanding, grace, and patience, both to yourself and to others.

Chapter 31: Get Started

They say later in life, you won't most regret what you did—you'll most regret what you didn't do, what you didn't try. Whatever it is you want to do in life, get started. You'll most likely never feel 100% confident, fully ready, or know every single detail. Fear will show up. Don't let that stop you. If you wait until you're completely ready in every way, you'll likely never start. Take a step. Take a little action. Get the ball rolling. Have faith you'll figure it out as you go. You don't need to have it all figured out. Take a leap of faith—faith in yourself, faith in people, faith in a higher power.

Sometimes starting feels overwhelming—maybe it's completely cutting out a habit or diving into a big new step. Instead, start small. Take one little step. Cut down a bit instead of completely cutting out. Progress, even small progress, compounds over time and leads to massive achievements and improvements. Want to read? Pick up the book. Want to write? Pick up the pen. Want to go for a run? Put on your shoes. Wanna diet? Cut down a few candy bars, not all. Once you start, momentum builds. Small steps create movement, and movement creates results. Don't overwhelm yourself by treating it like an emergency. Don't overthink it. Focus on what you *can* do right now, not on what you can't control.

Dream big. Embrace uncertainty. There's magic in chasing the unknown. Shoot for the stars. Put in the effort, and the universe will gravitate toward you. Enjoy the process, enjoy the thrill, embrace challenges with confidence, and appreciate every bit of progress. Take action, even if it's just a little. Your thoughts and feelings won't always align with your values or beliefs—but courage doesn't require perfection. One small step can influence your thoughts, feelings, and situation. Actions, thoughts, feelings—they all influence one another.

Believe. Achieve. Reach for the stars. Shrinking yourself does no one any favors. We all have immense potential. We were made to manifest greatness if we choose to. Start now. Start small. Start today.

Book recommendations:

- The power of your subconscious mind. Joseph Murphy.

- Mind over mood. Dennis Greenberger. Christine Padesky.

- I can't make this up. Kevin Hart

- Don't sweat the small stuff, it's all small stuff. Richard Carlson.

- As a man thinketh. James Allen.

- Start something that matters. Blake Mycoskie.

- It's not over until you win. Les Brown.

- Stoicism. Matthew Van Natta.

- How to win friends and influence people. Dale Carnegie.

- Public speaking for success. Dale Carnegie.

- Cry like a man. Jason Wilson.

About the author:

Sakariya A Hirad is a great thinker and a kind soul. He's 23, his life journey is not of the ordinary. He has a history of issues with his mental health and addiction. He is currently still incarcerated in where he started his journey as an author and to be a better healthier man than he once was. He's born and raised in Columbus, Ohio, where he also lives. He also appreciates grace big time, hopes to inspire and express the greater image of our humanity.

Email: hbkfrenchy@gmail.com /Instagram: @bankroll_zak

www.ingramcontent.com/pod-product-compliance
Lightning Source LLC
Chambersburg PA
CBHW020421150626
46554CB00014B/2316